First edition published 2017
Printed in United States
23 22 21 20 19 18 17   1 2 3 4 5 6 7 8

For the Beauty of the Earth
Written by Folliot S. Pierpoint
Design by Mighty Media
Illustrations by Lucy Fleming

Library of Congress Cataloging-in-Publication Data

Names: Pierpoint, Folliot Sandford, 1835-1917, author. | Fleming, Lucy, illustrator. | Kocher, Conrad, 1786-1872, composer.
Title: For the beauty of the Earth / by Folliot S. Pierpoint ; illustrated by Lucy Fleming.
Description: First edition. | Minneapolis, MN : Sparkhouse Family, 2017. | Includes musical notation of setting by Conrad Kocher.
Identifiers: LCCN 2016032669 | ISBN 9781506421834 (hardcover : alk. paper)
Subjects: LCSH: Hymns, English--Juvenile.
Classification: LCC M2196.P54 F6 2017 | DDC 264/.23--dc23
LC record available at https://lccn.loc.gov/2016032669

VN0004589; 9781506421834; NOV2016

Sparkhouse Family
510 Marquette Avenue
Minneapolis, MN 55402
sparkhouse.org

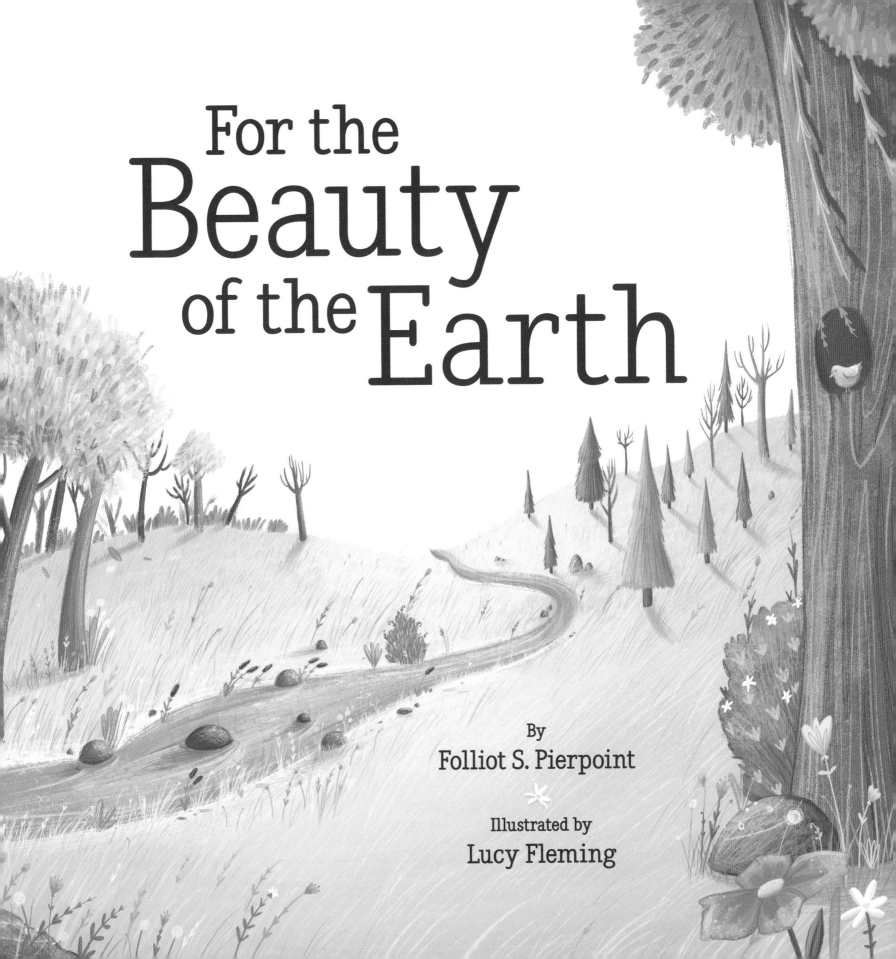

For the
Beauty
of the Earth

By

Folliot S. Pierpoint

Illustrated by

Lucy Fleming

For the beauty of the earth,
for the glory of the skies,

for the love which from our birth
over and around us lies;

Lord of all, to thee we raise
this our hymn of grateful praise.

For the beauty
of each hour

of the day and
of the night,

hill and vale, and tree and flower,

sun and moon, and stars of light;

Lord of all, to thee we raise
this our hymn of grateful praise.

For the joy of ear and eye,
for the heart and mind's delight,

for the mystic harmony,
linking sense to sound and sight;

Lord of all, to thee we raise
this our hymn of grateful praise.

For the joy of
human love,

brother, sister,
parent, child,

friends on earth and friends above,
for all gentle thoughts and mild;

Lord of all,
to thee we raise

this our hymn
of grateful praise.

For thy church, that evermore
lifteth holy hands above,

offering up on every shore
her pure sacrifice of love;

Lord of all, to thee we raise
this our hymn of grateful praise.

For thyself, best Gift Divine
to the world so freely given,
for that great, great love of thine,
peace on earth, and joy in heaven;

Lord of all, to thee we raise
this our hymn of grateful praise.

For the Beauty of the Earth

Folliott S. Pierpoint, 1864

Conrad Kocher, 1838

1. For the beau - ty of the earth for the beau - ty of the sky,
2. For the beau - ty of each hour of the day and of the night,
3. For the joy of ear and eye, for the heart and mind's de - light,
4. For the joy of hu - man love, broth - er sis - ter, par - ent child,
5. For each per - fect gift of thine to our race so free - ly giv'n,

for the love which from our birth o - ver and a - round us lies,
hill and vale, and tree and flow'r, sun and moon and stars of light,
for the mys - tic har - mo - ny link - ing sense o sound and sight,
friends on earth and friends a - bove, for all gen - tle thoughts and mild,
gra - ces hu - man and di - vine, flow'rs of earth and buds of heav'n,

Lord of all to Thee we raise, This our hymn of grate - ful - praise.